A Letter t

Dear Reader,

We unpack the family ornaments from the attic, we acquire a tree and string lights. We sing carols at church and in the car. We get out the recipes that came from Grandma and bake sweets we only eat once a year.

All of this seasonal magic takes preparation—presents are thoughtfully selected, purchased, and wrapped. The calendar requires careful attention, in order to juggle Christmas gatherings and extra commitments. The grocery list is carefully curated to make sure you forget none of the family favorites. If you're really good, you'll do all of this before the mall and the baking aisle of the grocery story look like the "after" scene from an apocalypse movie.

I've been thinking about what it means to prepare. Both Advent and Lent are seasons of preparation in the Christian calendar and faith, but they are different kinds of preparation. In Advent we are preparing to receive something vulnerable—a baby, yes, but also a God who dared to be made flesh. How do we prepare to receive the divine gift of vulnerability and then turn to seeing and advocating for those whom are vulnerable in our world?

What if we were to prepare for more than just the festivity and presents and lights? What if we prepared to welcome the Christ child into our lives and prepared enough room for him to stay after the tree is on the curb and the decorations are back in storage? What if *this* Advent we opened our hearts and prepared enough room to receive not just the baby sweet and mild in the manger, but the man and ministry that changed the world and has the ability to change our lives?

Prepare: An Advent Devotional has been written by young pastors from the Bethany Fellowship to be just that—a chance to pause, to look toward the hope we have in Jesus Christ, to be centered in prayer as a way to be transformed and then challenged to live as though the baby in the manger all those years ago can crack open our way of seeing and being in the world; that we might be challenged to see God as vulnerable in the Christ child, but also see God's vulnerability in our neighbor, in our community, and in those we consider invisible, unseen, unheard.

Each day will offer an excerpt from a larger passage of scripture; we encourage you as part of your daily reflection to read the larger passage, to engage the good word of the coming of Christ Jesus in our midst this season. The scripture passages for the candlelighting services center around the Gospel of Matthew. We hope that you are enriched by our offering,

Blessings,
Cara Gilger

Prepare

AN
ADVENT DEVOTIONAL

THE BETHANY FELLOWS
CARA GILGER, EDITOR

chalice
press

Saint Louis, Missouri

An imprint of Christian Board of Publication

Cover art: Adobe Stock

ChalicePress.com

PRINT: 9780827231825
EPUB: 9780827231832
EPDF: 9780827231849

Printed in the United States of America

Prepare

AN
ADVENT DEVOTIONAL

THE BETHANY FELLOWS
CARA GILGER, EDITOR

CONTENTS

Hope

Keeping Watch

Read Matthew 24:36–44.

"Therefore keep watch, because you do not know on what day your Lord will come." (Matthew 24:42, NIV)

Advent is the state of expectation, a "hoping for." If we hope to see Jesus, then shouldn't the way we live our lives prepare us for such an encounter? We don't know when this divine encounter will take place, so shouldn't we always be preparing, always watching? The gospels tells us who Jesus is in our midst: Jesus is the marginalized. He is the poor. He is the sick. He is the blind. He is the dark-skinned immigrant man at the border. He is the marginalized in our midst. Perhaps this Advent as we prepare, we can perhaps become intentional about seeing Jesus in our brothers and sisters who are marginalized, who live in the margins of our awareness.

I want to invite you to practice seeing Jesus in every marginalized person you meet and know. How you respond to them–your inner thoughts, your actions, and your words–is a reflection of how you will respond to Jesus. This season of Advent is a time to prepare, *to watch*–and you are invited to tend to the places in your heart and mind that prevent you from seeing the beauty in those in the margins. You are invited to sit in your truth so that love can guide you in a new way.

Dear God, let love guide me to the path where I can see Jesus in all people–especially those the in the margins.

Turning Our Hope

Read Psalm 25:1–10.

Guide me in your truth. Teach me.
You are God my Savior.
I put my hope in you all day long. (Psalm 25:5, NIRV)

In whom do we place our trust? As a faithful Christian I want to say, "God through Christ Jesus," loud and proud. But that would be dishonest to the other part of me—the part of me that places my hope in other sources rather than God; the part of me that places my hope in my own abilities and privileges, that places hope in my work and my economic value and in what I achieve.

That kind of hope is real, but it is a hope that is not concerned for my neighbor. Where we place our hope shapes who we imagine has access to goodness and compassion. We place our hope in systems, relationships, and ideas that not only do not match up with what the gospel teaches us about Jesus, but keep us from seeing all the goodness that God has for us, for our neighbor, for the kin-dom of God. During the Advent season we are invited to reorient our hope away from places of power and toward the manger, where God sent his son to teach us where our hope should lie and how that hope ought to shape us toward compassion and grace.

Holy One, turn me toward a hope that is ground in you, rather than in things that slip away, that don't consider my neighbor or distract me from your truth.

For Whom

Read Jeremiah 33:14–16.

In those days and at that time I will cause a righteous Branch to spring up for David; and he shall execute justice and righteousness in the land. (Jeremiah 33:15)

We live in a time where we cannot seem to agree on *what and for whom* justice and righteousness should be. Indeed, disagreements over this fundamental moral and spiritual question cause our government to gridlock again and again. Yet the Bible offers clear and consistent direction about *what and for whom* justice and righteousness are. After all, our risen Christ and savior, our brother and teacher Jesus, was a brown-skinned Palestinian man from, of all places, Nazareth.

We follow Jesus, who was born in a barn to an unwed teenage mother. Jesus, whose family fled as refugees to Egypt. Jesus, who shared food with prostitutes, tax collectors, and social outcasts; who healed the mentally and physically ill; who touched the ritually pure and impure. Jesus, who kept and broke sabbath laws. Jesus, who taught love, not just for family and friends, but for strangers, foreigners, and even enemies. Jesus, who was crucified because he threatened the political and religious powers that be. We follow Jesus, the righteous Branch, the man whose life and death show us *what and for whom* justice and righteousness are. As we prepare for Jesus' birth, let us proclaim the liberating righteousness and justice that he lived and taught.

Holy God, give us hearts to experience the liberation from sin and suffering that your righteousness and justice offer all of us. Amen.

Imagining God's Promise

Read Isaiah 2:1-5.

They will beat their swords into plowshares and their spears into pruning hooks. Nation will not take up sword against nation, nor will they train for war anymore. (Isaiah 2:4b, NIV)

Where is the line between hope and delusion? We average nearly one mass shooting a day in America. We've been involved in some armed conflict for roughly 90 percent of our nation's existence. Violence that tears apart families and rends communities is so ingrained in the social fabric of our culture, it is difficult to imagine life without it. In most circles, including the Church, we have stopped trying. "Swords into plowshares" sounds more like delusion than hope. In this scripture, Isaiah's prophecy comes to a wayward people who have, similar to us, made gods of many things other than YHWH. And yet, Isaiah insists on this vision of hope—not as a wish, but as a certain reality.

The prophet possesses a different kind of vision; he sees the world as it is, but also possesses the prophetic imagination to articulate a vision of God's promises. Though they often tell deeply uncomfortable truths about us, we could not do without the prophets' insistence on hope, rooted in a deep faith in God's ultimate power to determine the future. In the midst of our brokenness, we desperately need someone who can see beyond what we see; without that vision, we might be abandoned to cynicism. At Advent, we renew our hope, looking through the eyes of the prophets to grasp the hope that ultimately animates our lives.

Lord, in the midst of my despair, give me eyes to see beyond what is, to what you have promised will be. Amen.

Creating Space

Read Psalm 122.

For the sake of my relatives and friends,
I will say, "Peace be within you." (Psalm 122:8)

Having peace is not as complicated as we sometimes make it. Though we may not always realize it, we already have peace. I believe peace is part of our DNA and life force. While this may seem far-fetched, take a quick journey with me to understand how.

Think of a moment when you have settled down after a long day of activity. The space you are in is quiet. Your thoughts begin to slow down. You close your eyes, take a few deep breaths, and finally release a sigh of relief. That is peace. It didn't take a great deal of time or effort to arrive there, but it *did* take awareness and discipline.

I believe this was the psalmist's objective when he spoke of peace in the text. He wasn't sending peace or giving peace. It was as if he was saying: "May the peace within you be activated." When that peace is activated, our ability to withstand is strengthened. Our ability to help others discover their peace is strengthened. As that peace is activated, hope has the capability to last longer, no matter what the world is around us.

During the impatient moments of waiting, during the unknown moments of wandering and the chaotic moments of what's next, help us activate the peace within.

Light in the Dark

Read Romans 13:11–14.

[T]he night is far gone, the day is near. Let us then lay aside the works of darkness and put on the armor of light. (Romans 13:12)

Ah, the dangers of navigating a dark room. And what a difference even a bit of light makes! A light unto our feet helps us to avoid those things that would cause us to trip and stumble. And so it is in all aspects of our living; we need a way of seeing clearly those things that can cause harm to us and others. And when we prepare a way for Christ to be born into our lives, we invite a light by which we can address those things that keep us from the flourishing to which God calls creation.

Let us carry the hope this season that God will bring light into even the darkest corners of our living. Let the festive holiday lights serve to remind you that Christ is a bearer of light unto the world. And don't be surprised if you find yourself singing along with the songs of the season: "A thrill of hope, the weary world rejoices / For yonder breaks a new and glorious morn!"

Great Giver of Light, may we see our living with the clarity that comes from living in your ways. Give us the courage to address that which your light exposes, so that we may truly flourish in your new and glorious morn.

Hungering for Hope

Read Micah 5:2–5a.

And he shall stand and feed his flock in the strength of the LORD…
[A]nd he shall be the one of peace. (Micah 5:4a, 5a)

It is difficult to hope, or do much of anything, when you are hungry. Most of us have had the experience of being *hangry*– when a delayed snack or meal causes us to be easily irritable, impatient, or angry. Hunger, which has been shown to impact mood, ability to concentrate and even one's ability to think straight, is an everyday reality for more than 800 million people around the world. Hunger and malnutrition are responsible for the highest mortality rate in children and long-lasting physiological, social and cognitive effects on developing minds and bodies.

Micah's promise to the people of Israel of a leader who will come and "feed his flock in the strength of the LORD," is a promise for justice. Imagine a leader who vowed to feed all of our nation's people–who would ensure that young and old alike would have enough to eat. This first step toward justice *is possible* in our world, where there *is enough* food for all. This Advent season, let us not only hope for such a world but actively serve as the hands and feet that make such a world reality.

O God, to those who have hunger, give bread.
And to us who have bread, give the hunger for justice.
–Prayer from Latin America

Prayer

Tell the Truth in Prayer

Read Matthew 3:1–12.

In those days John the Baptist came, preaching in the wilderness of Judea and saying, "Repent, for the kingdom of heaven has come near." (Matthew 3:1–2, NIV)

When we pray, it is believed that we are talking to God. I imagine it's a time when you bring all of your truth to God. All of your being to the Creator. All of your struggles to the Holy One. All of what makes you you, to a God of love and grace. We all have our own biases against another. We are all socialized to see each one another as "other." Whether its racism, sexism, xenophobia, or homophobia…all of us struggle with bias. Yet the scripture reminds us that we can bring all of who we all to God in prayer.

When you pray, it's a time to talk with a God who knows your very hearts and still receives you as God's very own. This Advent, I invite you to the prayer room in faith. I want to invite you to a level of truth and faith that lends itself to transformation. As we prepare in this season, let us prepare by bringing those secret thoughts about others   to prayer. Let prayer become a space of repentance. Letting go of ideologies that keep us from seeing God in each other only happens when we first admit how broken and shattered we are. God can handle our brokenness. God can help us see in our blindness. Let this be a season of hard-truth prayer time. Let us pray about our biases and those things that keep us from seeing God in each other.

Dear God, help me see anew your people with the heart of love you possess for your whole creation.

Called by Name

Read Isaiah 55:1–5.

Come, all you who are thirsty,
come to the waters;
and you who have no money,
come, buy and eat! (Isaiah 55:1a NIV)

This portion of the book of Isaiah is written to a people exiled by the Babylonians, returning to the land of Judah. How do an exiled people maintain their identity as a minority, as strangers in a strange land? They remember that they are God's chosen people, even as they are displaced from the land. Observing the Law, for Israel, was a practiced inoculation against the temptation to mirror the culture in which they lived. In the gospels, Jesus critiques religious leaders who have had their identity swallowed up by the values (and convenience) of life under Roman rule.

In the same breath, the prophet both comforts the people–reminding them of God's provision as they enter a new reality–while also reminding them that they are not called to values that mirror those of the culture they are leaving behind. They are *God's* people. This is an identity to be both practiced and nurtured. We who find ourselves in a culture with values that do not mirror our own are called not only to trust in God's promises, but to practice and nurture our identity as God's people. In order to remind ourselves of our deep and lasting connection with God, who has claimed us as God's own, we go into prayer, into an Advent season that reminds us that we are not what we have been and that the new world that is coming will not be as the one we presently inhabit.

Lord, draw me near to you, in the midst of this season; remind me that you called me by name and you are mine. Amen.

Worry and Wonder

Read Philippians 4:4–6.

Do not worry about anything, but in everything by prayer and supplication with thanksgiving let your requests be made known to God. (Philippians 4:6)

I am a natural born worrier. I could fill the rest of this book with a list of worries–some deeply personal and real, some frivolous and silly. As much as I wish these worries didn't shape my life, they do.

Worry grounds us in fear. It tells us that the world is a scary place, people are untrustworthy, we should look out for ourselves, we should think small. The gift of Advent, the gift of the Christ child, is that in his birth we are invited to turn our fear into a sense of wonder. We see this holy compost happen throughout the Christmas story–Joseph fear turns to wonder at God's goodness and Mary's faithfulness, the fearful shepherds wonder at the manger, and the wise men allow their curiosity and wonder to lead them to discover a child under a star.

When we suspend our worry and fear about our lives, of other people, and of the world around, we leave room for God's holy wonder to surprise us with grace, mercy, and goodness.

Wondrous Creator, teach us to see our lives and your world with a wonder that erases our worry and orients us to your possibility.

Together We See

Read Isaiah 40:1–11.

The Lord's glory will appear,
*   and all humanity will see it together;*
*   the Lord's mouth has commanded it. (Isaiah 40:5, CEB)*

We must admit that so many of the words that come out of our mouths are empty: Words that are not helpful or encouraging. Words that may even be insulting and disparaging. But when the Lord speaks the words we read in the Bible or hear through the sermons and songs of others, we anticipate words of hope, inspiration, comfort, and grace.

When the Lord speaks, we expect that the Lord's words will be true and dependable. When the Lord commands that the Lord's glory will appear and all humanity will see it together, we are in awe of this promise because of the "here and not yet" nature of it. We simultaneously hope *and* trust that, when the Lord's glory does appear in our lives, in our churches, in our communities, all of humanity will see it together and we will be forever changed, for "the Lord's mouth has commanded it."

Glorious Lord, thank you for speaking words that command that we see you and that we see you together. These days, it is often hard to imagine all of humanity seeing anything as one, but your words give us hope. We pray that we may see your glory all around, and that all of humanity will indeed see your glory together and be transformed by it.

Drawing the Circle Wide

Read Romans 15:4–13.

Welcome one another, therefore, just as Christ has welcomed you, for the glory of God. (Romans 15:7)

Advent is often a time of preparing to open our homes to neighbors, friends, and family. We welcome new visitors in our churches during this season of preparation. Hospitality is a central piece of our faith lives, a call to welcome at church, yes, and beyond the church walls. Whether at church , home, or in works of justice, hospitality is at the heart of what and how we live. Time and time again in our sacred text, we are reminded not just to welcome those we know but also to welcome the stranger. When Paul implores us to welcome one another, he is not writing anything new, but a needed reminder.

We need this reminder to welcome one another, not only in our physical lives, but in our prayer lives as well. During this season when we welcome people, well-known *and* new, let us take time in prayer to ask who we are overlooking, unintentionally or not, because when we extend welcome we welcome the Christ child into our midst.

In our time with God, may we bless not only those whom we welcome with open arms, but the stranger and those we find it hard to love. Prayers are powerful, and, thanks be to God, powerful enough to change us.

God who draws the circle wide, may I welcome with your generous Spirit all I meet this day.

Seeing the Impossible

Read Isaiah 11:1–10.

The spirit of the LORD shall rest on him,
the spirit of wisdom and understanding,
the spirit of counsel and might,
the spirit of knowledge and the fear of the LORD...
They will not hurt or destroy
on all my holy mountain;
for the earth will be full of the knowledge of the LORD
as the waters cover the sea. (Isaiah 11:2, 9)

Prayer is not easily defined or measured. Our prayers can sometimes feel like a leap in the dark, flung out in hope to the unknown. Similarly, waiting in preparation can be a maddening time of work with seemingly no results. Yet after a period of waiting is over, after prayers have been answered (often in ways we could not have even imagined), we see the wisdom of the unknown time.

Instead of answers in this season, what if we prayed for the Spirit to be upon one another and ourselves? The Spirit of wisdom and understanding, counsel and might, knowledge and fear of the Lord. What fruits will be produced when we shift from "answers on demand" to Spirit-filled insight? Isaiah gives us quite the vision of the seemingly impossible: the wolf living with the lamb, the cow and the bear grazing together, and a little child leading the way. Through Christ, all things are possible; may we follow the little child in the waiting and preparation.

Spirit of the living God, fall afresh on me, grant me wisdom and understanding to see the impossible made possible through you. Amen.

Making a Way

Read Psalm 34:1–8.

O taste and see that the LORD is good;
happy are those who take refuge in him. (Psalm 34:8)

I have heard it said that hope is the recollection of the past appropriated in the future. That was certainly the case for David. He recalled the ways that the Lord had delivered him from his fears. He evoked the memory of the times that the Lord had saved him from every trouble. And his memories were quite enough of a precedent for him to boast in the Lord. But God's saving acts go far beyond the experiences of David's past; we hear time and time again throughout scripture how God has made a way for his people. Perhaps God has made a way for you, too.

Relationships of love and trust are built upon our experiences. Can you name the ways that the Lord has come to your aid? Who else has tasted and seen that the Lord is good?

Let us not forget to recall the ways that God has come to our succor. Our recollection of the past is surely hope enough for the future, as we await the birth of the Christ child.

God of ages past, God of what is yet to come, I recall the ways that you have cared for your people and for me. May I carry these memories into an unknown future, trusting that you will continue to work toward our wholeness.

Change

Clearing the Way

Read Matthew 11:2–11.

*"I will send my messenger ahead of you,
 who will prepare your way before you." (Matthew 11:10b, NIV)*

It is the dead of winter, but come spring I will spend time in the garden bagging leaves, cutting back dead limbs, and turning the soil to prepare the way for new growth to spring forth. Part of preparing is clearing away the dead things in your life that no longer serve you, so that new things can take hold and root deeply.

Advent is a season of such clearing and rooting. In our passage from Matthew, Jesus tells the messenger of John to "Go back and report to John what you hear and see: The blind receive sight, the lame walk, those who have leprosy are cleansed, the deaf hear, the dead are raised, and the good news is proclaimed to the poor" (vv. 4–5, NIV). The baby born in the manger grew in strength and wisdom to be a Messiah who invites us to clear out our sinful ways of being in the world and let take root compassion, justice, mercy, and love.

God of New Beginnings, root deeply in me your word, so that I may be transformed to be not just a hearer but a doer of your good news.

Blind Spots

Read Psalm 146:5–10.

[T]he LORD opens the eyes of the blind.
The LORD lifts up those who are bowed down. (Psalm 146:8a)

To what are you "blind"–unable or unwilling to see? Where are you bowed down by wounds or trauma that need God's healing?

Since my daughter's birth, my blind spots and deepest wounds have risen to the surface. Attending to these blind spots and wounds has been painful, difficult, inconvenient, and sometimes even ugly work. It has required me to see parts of myself that I have long buried in shame, anger, blame, fear, despair, and loneliness. But my eyes have also been opened to see that those same parts carry beauty, courage, strength, the resolve to live, and the desire to be lifted up. I have been learning and relearning to respond to my blindness, shame, and wounds with empathy and compassion; to sit with the angry, fearful, and sad parts of myself and invite God in.

One of the things I have heard over and over again these last months is that the birth of a child often reveals our blind spots and wounds. Well, friends, it is Advent, and we are *all* expecting the birth of a baby. A baby who will change everything. A baby who will reveal our blind spots and wounds, who will open our eyes and lift us up. A baby who invites us from death to life.

Holy God, prepare us for the birth of Immanuel. Open our eyes. Lift us up. Heal and transform us.

Singing a New Song

Read Luke 1:46b–55.

"He has brought down rulers from their thrones
but has lifted up the humble.
He has filled the hungry with good things
but has sent the rich away empty." (Luke 1:52–53, NIV)

Think Bob Dylan, in 1963, giving voice to a generation hostile to those in power with "The Times They Are A-Changin'." Think Sam Cooke, infuriated by his experience of segregation on tour, proclaiming that "A Change Is Gonna Come." Think Marvin Gaye, in 1971, against the backdrop of police brutality during an anti-war protest, asking "What's Going On?" Think of a young woman, probably an adolescent, sitting in her cousin's home and singing of God's justice in the past tense—she doesn't say what God will do or might do or could do, she sings about what God has already done.

A change is not coming; it *has* come. God has moved on behalf of the poor and oppressed. That is the revolutionary, counter-cultural news of Christmas, the radical message of Mary's protest song. The call for those who gather to celebrate it is *not* to be ready for something that is coming, but to join ourselves with something that has already begun—to join a movement on behalf of the misfits, and to sing our songs of hope and peace and joy as a means of resisting what the world seems to be currently telling us about who holds power and who deserves justice and who can belong. A change has come, and it is this change that will ultimately change us.

Lord, help me to embrace the change you have already made on behalf of the oppressed.

Patience

Read James 5:7–10.

The farmer waits for the precious crop from the earth, being patient with it until it receives the early and the late rains. You also must be patient. (James 5:7b–8a)

I would imagine that you have, at some time, embarked on a voyage during which you heard, if not spoken, the timeless question, "Are we there yet?" You have also likely noticed that the phrase often seems less an inquiry and more an indictment of the present moment; an expression of our restlessness to be somewhere else.

What are you doing about your inner restlessness? Perhaps we could make room for a daily routine or discipline that would develop our patience? After all, patience isn't an instant virtue any more than doing one sit up will give you instant six-pack abs. And while abs of steel would be a nice thing to have, patience is something we cannot do without! Here's why: the beautiful–but challenging–work of bearing God's love and justice in the world will require it of us (just as it was required of the prophets of old).

Are we there yet? No. Take a deep breath and settle in. Let us follow in the footsteps of the prophets, engaging each present moment as agents of transformation for God's divine purposes in the world, strengthening our hearts with patience for that blessed work.

Holy One, may patience be a close companion in the work to which you have called us.

A Wonderful Change

Read 1 Corinthians 1:3–9.

I give thanks to my God always for you because of the grace of God that has been given you in Christ Jesus, for in every way you have been enriched in him. (1 Corinthians 1:4–5a)

"A wonderful change has come over me." These are lyrics of the song "A Wonderful Change," written by Walter Hawkins. It illustrates what happens when Christ enters our life. There is newness and determination to fulfill God's call, because of the change in heart, mind, and soul.

Paul's words to the Corinthians are exciting, sincere, and as beautiful as the song lyric above. He is excited about the grace given and the way lives have been enriched by Christ, because Paul himself has experienced this. What a positive perspective on change. Ironically, some people do not view change positively, but view it with hesitation and anxiety—wondering if they'll make the right decision, what others may think, and if they can maintain the change.

There is solace in knowing:

1. Change is possible through God's grace and life enrichment through Christ *is* the right decision.

2. We have God's help and Christ's power to live daily into the change.

And even if every day isn't so wonderful, the grace of God is sufficient to keep us.

May we continually view grace as the kindness of God to us, change as the love of God for us, and enrichment as the power of God in our lives.

Refined Anew

Read Malachi 3:1–4.

For he is like a refiner's fire... (Malachi 3:2c)

I grew up in the era of the "My Buddy" doll, with the commercial jingle during Saturday morning cartoons that went, "My buddy, my buddy, where I go he goes." Similarly, that was also the era during which I was taught that Jesus was also my very own best friend to tag along with me on all my adventures. This Jesus was loving, always there, and affirming of me.

It didn't take me long into young adulthood to understand that Jesus was more than a buddy to tag along with me on all my various adventures. Instead, Jesus liked to show up and show off by teaching me how to love my enemies, by challenging the inherited biases and beliefs of my ancestors, and by teaching me hard and often painful truths about myself. As with the refiner's fire in Malachi, each time we learn a new, painful lesson, we are refined into a new creation. The beliefs, practices, and clutter that no longer serve us are stripped away. In their place we are left with a faith strengthened in ways that surprise and delight. Instead of a buddy, Jesus is our guiding star, leading us to and through new and challenging places.

This Advent, refine us to be followers of Jesus, O God, by guiding us to follow your holy light to the uncomfortable and clarifying places you call us.

Ready and Joyful

Read Psalm 51:10–12.

Create in me a clean heart, O God,
and put a new and right spirit within me.
Do not cast me away from your presence,
and do not take your holy spirit from me.
Restore to me the joy of your salvation,
and sustain in me a willing spirit. (Psalm 51:10–12)

Are you ready? A three-word question with a myriad of possible perspectives. One can be "ready" to go. One can "ready" to stay. One can be "ready" to sing or read or be silent. One can be "ready" to start a new regimen.

Regardless of what the question pertains to, the answer should be fully considered. Answering the question of, "Are you ready?" involves more than a simple yes or no. It is, more importantly, about action. Once you say yes, the clock starts ticking. And, also, with no, the clock ticks, awaiting the yes.

In this passage, we see the psalmist answered the question of ready with YES. The beauty of it is that the psalmist knew what he was ready for—a clean heart, a right and willing spirit, God's Spirit (presence) and joy.

The psalmist was ready for change—specific change. This change was from the inside out. It was the kind of change that would allow the psalmist to be a better person for himself and for the call of God.

Are you ready? For specific change? Are you ready for your heart and spirit to be cleaned and willing? Are you ready for continual joy and the presence of God? If not, get ready. Prepare yourself for an amazing change that will lead to an amazing life... Though it will have challenges, it will nonetheless be amazing!

O God, in this season of tradition, open my heart to the changes you are calling me to make. Deepen my joy for you and restore my spirit.

Live

Shared Ground

Read Matthew 1:18–25.

When Joseph woke up, he did what the angel of the Lord had commanded him and took Mary home as his wife. (Matthew 1:24, NIV)

Joseph has a choice to make that will affect his life forever. Will he stand with Mary or not? To say "yes" would be to compromise his reputation. He could not have known that it would mean being made a refugee by Herod's violent rampage, aimed at *his* child. This is leapt over in Scripture, but linger on it for a minute: Joseph, by choosing to stand with Mary, demonstrated a particular kind of love for her; and, by choosing to stand with Mary, he chose to stand with Jesus; by choosing to stand with Jesus, he stood for those for whom Jesus stood; by standing with those for whom Jesus stood, he stood for you. Joseph said, "Here. You can have my life, my pride, my reputation, my love." Because of his and Mary's collective vulnerability, we have come to know the profound love of God, who became vulnerable so that we might know that God stands with us.

In the vulnerability of this baby, God issues us the invitation to love God in kind. God loves us by standing with us this way, and we love God by standing with God's people. It's not only spiritual, but physical. Yes, it's about your heart and your mind, but it's more about your feet and the ground on which you choose to stand, and with whom you share that ground. Would you risk your reputation to stand for and with God's people? For the God who has shared ground with you in the vulnerability of a baby?

Lord, may my feet be ready to share ground with those who are vulnerable.

Flesh and Bone

Read Isaiah 7:13–16.

Look, the young woman is with child and shall bear a son, and shall name him Immanuel. He shall eat curds and honey. (Isaiah 7:14b–15a)

Bodies matter. *Your* body matters. This way of faith is not only for mind, spirit, heart, and soul. It is a way for the body. Because, bodies matter. This reading from Isaiah reminds us of the mundane, earthy, bodily way that God came to earth–growing in a young woman's womb, And then, like any child, delighting in delicious things to eat.

How might we live differently if we felt called to care for our bodies? I would drink more water and go outside more often. How might we live differently if we felt called to care for one another's bodies? How might our perspective on bodies shift if we regularly saw Jesus depicted as a brown Palestinian man? Might we understand that to say "Black Lives Matter" means that black bodies matter? Because, bodies *do* matter. Your body and mine. Black, brown, yellow, pink, and white bodies. Young and old bodies. Male, female, gender-queer, cis- and trans- bodies. Immanuel, God incarnate, fully divine and fully human, fully embodied, flesh and bone–because bodies matter.

Remind us, O Christ, that, like us, you delighted in food and wine, you laughed and wept, you touched those who were considered clean and unclean, and you experienced the pleasure and pain of embodied life. Bring us back to our bodies, with gentleness and loving care.

Wounded Joy

Read Psalm 80: 1–7, 17–19.

Restore us, O God;
   let your face shine, that we may be saved. (Psalm 80:3)

Despite the vivid colors of this Advent season, sometimes things are just "blue." We have all felt the deep pain of desperation and even deeper pain of God's silence. This season of Advent is a time of anticipation and waiting, and there's hardly anything encouraging about having to wait for God when we are grieving.

But when the going gets tough, the tough get to praying. And God does hear our prayers, as raw as they may be. God can handle your anger, your shame, your sadness, your fatigue.

So if by chance you find yourself out of touch with the joy of the season's songs, I would invite you to lift your grief to God. For, when we risk our venerable tears of lament, we, in turn, open ourselves to the God who risks vulnerable love—such as the kind of vulnerable love that will soon be born in a manger, in the darkness of night. And from that place of darkness will come our deliverance.

O God, search our hearts. See the wounds of our lives and hold our pain and grief close. We claim your promise to be our companion in bearing our grief this holiday season, trusting that you will make your face to shine upon us, that we may be saved.

Called to Belong

Read Romans 1:1–7.

And you also are among those Gentiles who are called to belong to Jesus Christ. (Romans 1:6, NIV)

"Called to belong." These words stand out, as a fully met expectation. No disappointment. No wonder as to whether belonging will happen. It will. It does. Additionally, the call to belong is not to anyone or anything. It is to Jesus Christ.

The desire to fit in, be seen and heard, is intense. Just as intense is the inverse response of rejection. The One to whom we are called to belong truly understands rejection. Yet Jesus continued to live life to the fullest. That's what our call of belonging to Jesus Christ is—living life to the fullest, with each blink and breath. It acknowledges we have the "Best of the best" on our side. It means we can mature without judgment.

How amazing to know we are privileged to belong to the Greatest. In essence, it doesn't matter if the world doesn't approve. That's not to whom we're called to belong. The world, from whom we had looked for approval, has been given the same call. All are invited to answer this call to belong, so we all can live our best lives now!

God, help us fully answer the call to belong. Show us how to live such full lives that we encourage others to answer the call.

Living Promise

Read 2 Peter 3:8–15.

But, in accordance with his promise, we wait for new heavens and a new earth, where righteousness is at home. (2 Peter 3:13)

Our scriptures are full of paradox. The realm of God is here and now, and not yet. We are waiting for the Christ child to come into our world anew, a child who was born thousands of years ago. We hear of the impossible, yet know through Christ all things are possible. We are already living embodied faith as we prepare to welcome Emmanuel, God-with-us.

In many ways, Advent may be seen as a time to focus on preparing to live and enact our faith in new ways *after* Jesus is born. Yet in our preparation for the one made flesh who comes to dwell among us and change everything, we cannot become complacent in the waiting. We are called to embody our faith now, we live into the promises of the new heaven and new earth now. We pray, we hope, we change now, knowing that, with the coming of the Christ child, all will change again. And we will be ready to live out that promise with *all* of who we are—mind, soul, *and body.*

God of promise, help us to embody your love, here and now, even as we wait for more to be revealed.

Embodied Faith

Read Isaiah 42:1–4.

But here is my servant, the one I uphold;
my chosen, who brings me delight.
I've put my spirit upon him;
he will bring justice to the nations. (Isaiah 42:1, CEB)

You are a servant. You are upheld by the Lord. You are the one who brings the Lord delight. Repeat that to yourself. *You are the one who brings the Lord delight.* Maybe you already knew this to be true. Maybe you have been struggling with believing this to be true about you. I do not know. But I do believe that these words were not just for that ancient prophet. I believe these words are for YOU.

If you have ever struggled with your identity in Christ, this is a good place to start to claim it as a servant, as one who is upheld by God, as one who brings the Lord delight, as one who embodies the Spirit of the Living God, and as one who will bring justice to the nations. This is who you are. Embrace it. Celebrate it. Live it.

God, who has created me and determined that I am good, thank you for calling forth my identity in you. Thank you for helping me to serve and to bring justice to my school, workplace, neighborhood, and even to my church. Thank you for choosing me and for delighting in me. Thank you for your love.

A New Day

Read Isaiah 42:5–9.

I, the LORD, have called you for a good reason.
I will grasp your hand and guard you,
and give you as a covenant to the people,
as a light to the nations,
to open blind eyes, to lead the prisoners from prison,
and those who sit in darkness from the dungeon.
(Isaiah 42:6–7, CEB)

There are so many mixed messages that we replay in our heads. Those messages come from insults on the playground when we were ten, or harsh words spoken to us by our parents when we did not get something right, or former friends whose words cut and left deep scars from which we have yet to recover. We replay these messages over and over because we usually have not heard enough positive messages to overcome the negative messages that seem to be programmed into our psyche. But today is a new day!

Today, by the power of the Holy Spirit and maybe with a good therapist or spiritual director, you have the power to reprogram whatever messages in your head have been holding you back, keeping you from living fully into God's plan for your life. Memorize the words in our verses today. Confess them as your truth. And in time, believe that those other mixed messages will be silenced.

Lord, today I confess that I am called for a good reason. I thank you for holding my hand and for guarding me. Thank you that I am the answer to someone's prayers and a light to the nations. Thank you that I will do the kind of good in the word that opens eyes and sets people free.

In the Flesh

Read John 1:1–5.

What has come into being in him was life, and the life was the life of all people. The light shines in the darkness, and the darkness did not overcome it. (John 1:3b–5)

I worked as a chaplain a few years ago. My first day as chaplain in the hospital I remember my supervisor telling me that, when I walked in a room, I literally became the Word as flesh to someone experiencing a very bad day. I was embodied hope. My body represented God. My body was the word of God for them.

That continues to resonate with me as I walk in the world. I am embodied hope, a representation of God in flesh. As we reflect in the Advent season, I invite you to be intentional about how you present your body to the world. How does the Word made flesh speak as the light that shines in these dark days when racism continues to permeate our very world? How are we embodied hope for the immigrant at the border? How are we the light in dark places at a time when innocent black bodies are murdered by the hands of police? This is not about politics. This is embodied hope I speak of. How are we, *together,* walking in the world as Word in flesh? How do we use the bodies God gave us to bring the kin-dom of God nearer? How do we create a world in which all bodies are honored and cared for? The world needs representation of God manifested every day in every way.

God, remind me to be your Word in flesh in every way.

Candlelighting Services

Reading:

"Keep awake therefore, for you do not know on what day your Lord is coming." (Matthew 24:42)

Reflection: We do not know the hour when we may meet the living Christ in our daily lives. But I know one thing for sure: staying in constant vigilance, awake 24/7, is not realistic. As we enter into this Advent season, preparing to meet the living Christ anew, perhaps the call to stay awake is a call to stay open and watchful. To take a moment to notice where God is already meeting you or where you long to be met. To notice who God may be working through, to be pushed to see God working through those we least expect.

Throughout this first week of Advent, take a moment to light the first Advent candle, to reflect on where you have seen hope this week *and* where you need to see hope, and to notice how God is preparing hope in you.

Lighting: We light this candle, the first candle of Advent, *in* hope and *with* hope. May we keep awake to the living Christ who is already among us.

Prayer: God of the watching and waiting, awaken us to see your hope in the world, and inspire us to be part of that hope—especially in this season of Advent. Amen.

Candlelighting Services

Reading:

*"Prepare the way of the Lord,
     make his paths straight." (Matthew 3:3b)*

Reflection: This season of Advent brings the chaos of planning and doing. As we prepare to receive the Christ child, give us eyes to see the brokenness and chaos of the world and the courage not to turn away from its pain. Give us the desire to see in the brokenness the holy potential for the kingdom of God. Let this time slow so that we might be able to cultivate a sense of gratitude, a practice of peace, and a response to the call to be peacemakers in a broken world.

Lighting: We light this candle, the second candle of Advent, as people who long for peace. May we prepare the path for the Prince of Peace to enter into our midst.

Prayer: God of hope and peace, we pray that in this season we transform to become not just receivers of your peace but peacemakers in the footsteps of Jesus. Amen.

Candlelighting Services

Reading:

*"See, I am sending my messenger ahead of you,
who will prepare your way before you." (Matthew 11:10b)*

Reflection: John the Baptist was called by God to prepare the way for the coming of Christ Jesus, to speak hard truths, to live a life shaped by the goodness of Christ's saving power and the challenge of his prophetic wisdom. On this third Sunday of Advent, let us see ourselves in the call of John the Baptist and celebrate with joy the challenge and call to proclaim the Christ that comes to us in flesh and blood in a manger to teach, preach, and proclaim God's goodness.

Lighting: We light this third candle of Advent, as a sure, steady promise of your joy in us and for us as we are called to serve and proclaim the Word.

Prayer: Meet us in the complicated space where joy resides, O God. Meet us in our grief for what has been lost and in our hope of what is to come in Christ Jesus.

Candlelighting Services

Reading:

But after he had considered this, an angel of the Lord appeared to him in a dream and said, "Joseph son of David, do not be afraid to take Mary home as your wife, because what is conceived in her is from the Holy Spirit." (Matthew 1:20, NIV)

Reflection: God calls Joseph into the deep vulnerability of love. To love Mary in this moment will require trust, risk, and the sacrifice of pride. To love the baby in her belly, the catalyst for uninvited upheaval in his life, will require humility, gentleness, and habitual generosity. This is the kind of love we prepare to practice during Advent: to embrace this coming child, who will bring both upheaval and meaning to our existence; and to re-orient ourselves toward trust, risk, and the sacrifice of pride. Let us pray that, as we approach Bethlehem, the love of God will grow in us, that we may share that love with a hurting world.

Lighting: We light this candle, the fourth candle of Advent, thankful for the light of love in our lives. May that grow in us as we prepare to welcome the Christ child.

Prayer: Loving God, help us to love you, and your children, with the vulnerability and passion with which you have loved us. Amen.

Candlelighting Services

Reading:

All this took place to fulfill what had been spoken by the Lord through the prophet:
"Look, the virgin shall conceive and bear a son,
and they shall name him Emmanuel,"
which means, "God is with us." (Matthew 1:22–24)

Reflection: So often we think of Christmas as a culmination of our Advent preparations, but theologian Howard Thurman says in his poem "The Work of Christmas" that when the angels, the kings, the shepherds, and the star are gone, that's when the work of Christmas begins. That's when we continue the actions of Emmanuel: engaging people from all walks of life, even, or maybe especially, those traditionally shunned; speaking truth to powerful people; feeding hungry families; helping the hurting; being a peacemaker. And all the while, God is still with us.

Lighting: We light this Christ candle in gratitude for God being with us in the person of Jesus, in the Holy Spirit, and in the people we meet each day.

Prayer: O holy child of Bethlehem, descend to us, we pray; cast out our sin, and enter in; be born in us today. We hear the Christmas angels the great glad tidings tell; O come to us, abide with us, our God, Emmanuel.

About the Contributors

Rev. Thandiwe Dale Ferguson says Advent has long been one of her favorite seasons, one in which we prepare for the birth of Christ in our world and in our personal lives. Thandiwe is blessed to serve a fun-loving and generous congregation in Loveland, Colorado, and to parent two-year-old Cora, who reminds her to live in the present moment, to laugh often and loudly, and to delight in creation.

Rev. Chris Furr has served churches in Burntwood, England, and Alexandria, Virginia, and is currently the Senior Minister at Covenant Christian Church (Disciples of Christ) in Cary, North Carolina. He lives in Cary with his wife, Katie, and their two sons.

Rev. Cara Gilger serves as a preacher and congregational consultant in the Dallas area helping churches align their practices and structures with their vision for how God is calling them to serve their communities. In her personal time, Cara is an uncoordinated fitness enthusiast, and enjoys reading and traveling with her partner, Tim, and their two daughters as they work on their goal of hiking every National Park.

Rev. Mollie Landers Hatt serves Lakewood United Church of Christ in Lakewood, Colorado, as Associate Pastor. She loves outdoor ministry and is passionate about building community and connecting to creation and the Creator. Mollie is a new mom to Eleanor, who is teaching her new ways to prepare—and then trust the Spirit.

Rev. Kevin Howe serves as Community Pastor at Harvard Avenue Christian Church in Tulsa, Oklahoma. Passionate for mission and outreach, he engages the congregation in the greater community and beyond. Some of his favorite activities involve making music, playing sports, and traveling with his wife, Jodi.

Rev. Raenisha Karim, known by most as Rae, is a writer, speaker, and creative soul. With her pen she ministers to people in a variety of ways—all to the glory of God.

Rev. Cherisna Jean-Marie is the Dean of Chapel at Bethany College in Bethany, West Virginia. She also serves as the Vice President for the Fellowship of Black Disciples Clergywomen, a nonprofit organization with the National Convocation of the Christian Church (Disciples of Christ).

Rev. Dr. Delesslyn A. Kennebrew, J.D., M.Div., is an inspirational writer, visionary strategist, and a disciple maker. She currently serves as the Regional Minister for New and Transforming Churches in the Greater Kansas City Region of the Christian Church (Disciples of Christ). Her prayer is for all believers to experience "Life, Love, Liberation, and Laughter in Christ."

About Bethany Fellowships

Since 1999, Bethany Fellowships has been encouraging young pastors in their earliest years of ministry. This ministry was born out of the intention of strengthening congregations of the Christian Church (Disciples of Christ) by helping newly ordained, young pastors transition from seminary to sustained congregational ministry with a strong and healthy pastoral identity. Research indicated one third of young ministers might leave congregational ministry in their first five years. The good news is that Bethany Fellowships is helping to change that reality for Disciples pastors and congregations.

In the fall of 2014, a Bethany Fellows Ecumenical group launched with the same mission to a wider group of young ministers, from a variety of denominations. Today, Bethany Fellowships celebrates the Disciples Bethany Fellows and Ecumenical Bethany Fellows, as well as having encouraged a similar ministry for those engaged in campus ministry and college chaplaincy.

The Bethany Fellowships ministry model provides four years of support and encouragement by offering two retreats each year and helping young pastors develop a rhythm of spiritual practices and patterns for a lifetime of ministry. While on retreat, the Fellows receive the prayerful support of experienced pastors/mentors and the encouragement of significant collegial relationships. The retreat also includes a visit with dynamic congregations and leaders, fueling creativity and insights to share with the Fellows' own congregations. Through Bethany Fellowships, young ministers are better able to navigate the beginnings of a pastoral vocation, as well as crucial young adult life transitions, building confidence and strengthening leadership.

Bethany Fellowships is also in partnership with the Pension Fund of the Christian Church, facilitating the peer group component of the Pension Fund's Excellence in Ministry program. The Excellence in Ministry pilot program seeks to reduce or alleviate some of the key financial pressures that inhibit effective pastoral leadership of early career ministers, and improve the financial literacy and management of leaders and their congregations through education.

More information can be found at bethanyfellows.org or by contacting Rev. Kim Gage Ryan, Director, 573.489.2729.

What if *this* Advent, we prepared enough room to receive not just the baby sweet and mild in the manger, but the man and ministry that changed the world and has the ability to change our lives?

In these daily devotions for the four weeks of Advent, be prepared to respond to the divine gift of vulnerability in the Christ child, yes, but also in our families, neighbors, churches, communities, and world. Written by young pastors from the Bethany Fellows, each five-minute devotion includes a scripture, a reflection, and a prayer to help us pause and ponder the life-changing message of God, made flesh.

Bonus Content: Extend the *Prepare* devotional experience into Sunday worship or home devotions with the special candlelighting services for each Sunday in Advent, plus one for Christmas Eve or Christmas Day.

Bethany Fellows from around the United States wrote the devotions in *Prepare*. Since 1999 Bethany Fellows has served congregations of the Christian Church (Disciples of Christ) by helping newly ordained, young pastors transition from seminary to sustained congregational ministry with a strong and healthy pastoral identity. An ecumenical Bethany group has been serving young pastors from various denominations since 2014.

Cara Gilger, editor, is an author, artist, and minister who has served churches in Texas, Tennessee, and Indiana for more than 15 years.

More Advent Resources from Chalice Press

Experience the story of Christmas like never before! More than 50 evocative illustrations and scriptural reflections for adults will draw you into the beloved story more deeply, inviting you to contemplate and color the miracle and message of Jesus' birth in Bethlehem.

Illustrations by Jesse Turri, Natalie Turri
Reflections by Christopher Rodkey
Coloring Advent 9780827203976

RELIGION / Holidays / Christmas & Advent

ISBN 978-0-827231-82-5

9 780827 231825 >

chalice press
You Want to Change the World. So Do We.